PC DESKTOP TE(DESKTOP SUPPO SPECIALIST, IT SERVICE DESK TECHNICIAN, HELP DESK ANALYST: JUST IN TIME REVISION GUIDE FOR SUCCESS AT ANY ICT SUPPORT JOB INTERVIEW

It's for these job interviews:

IT Support Specialist
IT Service Desk Technician
PC Support/Technical Support/IT Support
IT Service Desk Technician
Desktop Support Specialist

Why this book:

It will help you to convey powerful and useful information about various aspects of IT Support Specialist job to the employer successfully.

It gives readers the most important practical job related information for supporting various aspects of ICT (Information & Communication Technology):

ICT infrastructure Support (e.g. desktops, laptops, printers, scanners, connectivity, software, e-mail, etc.)
Desktop Support (hardware, software, OS, peripherals)
Troubleshooting PC hardware and software problems
Non Technical/ Personal/ HR interview

Try to be in parking lot an hour before the interview and use this time to read over this E-book. It has been well written to make it a very quick read. Practicing with this interview questions and answers in the mirror will help with your replies to questions and pass with flying colors. It also covers non-technical, HR and Personnel questions in brief.

Good Luck,

Kumar

INDEX

SAS

ECC

BNC

PERFORMANCE OF MEMORY

DDR2-SDRAM

NORTHBRIDGE/SOUTHBRIDGE CHIPSET ARCHITECTURE

World Wide Name (WWN)

PORTS

IPCONFIG

SATA

HDMI

EMI

802.11g

WPA2

SMTP

USB

HYPER-THREADING

RAMBUS

MOTHERBOARD FORM FACTORS

BNC

DB25

BUS POWER

TROJAN HORSE

VPN

PCMCIA

CPU CACHE

RS232 CABLE PINOUTS

ZIF SOCKET

BOTNET

MALWARE

IP ADDRESS CLASSES

MAC ADDRESS FORMAT

MULTICAST

UNICAST

BROADCAST

IPV6

LOOP BACK ADDRESS

THE STANDARD PORTS

TRACERT

DSL

QUAD-CORE PROCESSOR

BLUE SCREEN OF DEATH

LGA 775

LGA 1155

RJ-11

RJ-45

TRANSMISSION CIRCUITS

PRINTER TYPES

SAFE MODE

RECOVERY CONSOLE

BIOS

CMOS

POST

COMPUTER PARTS

OSI

DEVICE MANAGER ERROR CODES

IRQ

Non Technical/ Personal/ HR   interview

Bottom Line Job interview?

Interview Question?

What are your greatest strengths?

What are your greatest weaknesses?

Had you failed to do any work and regret?

Where do you see yourself five years from now?

How Will You Achieve Your Goals?

Why are you leaving Your Current position?

Why are you looking for a new job?

Why should I hire you?

Aren't you overqualified for this position?

Describe a Typical Work Week?

Are You Willing to Travel?

Describe the pace at which you work?

How Did You Handle Challenges?

How do you handle pressure? Stressful situations?

How Many Hours Do You Work?

Why are you the best person for the job?

What are you looking for in a position?

What do you know about our organization?

What are your short term goals?

What Salary are you looking for?

Tell me more about yourself.

Why did you leave your previous job?

What relevant experience do you have?

If your previous co-workers were here, what would they say about you?

Where else have you applied?

What motivates you to do a good job?

Are you good at working in a team?

Has anything ever irritated you about people you've worked with?

Is there anyone you just could not work with?

Tell me about any issues you've had with a previous boss.

Do you have any questions?

Why did you choose this career?

What did you learn from your last job experience?

How do you keep current and informed about your job and the industries that you have worked in?

Tell me about a time when you had to plan and coordinate a project from start to finish?

What kinds of people do you have difficulties working with?

What do you want to be in 5 years?

Explain an Ideal career for you?

What are your job responsibilities?

What is your dream job?

What skills you have?

What sets you apart?

If the project not gone as planned what action you will take?

What you do if you are unable to meet deadlines?

Interpersonal skill?

Improve?

What do you feel has been your greatest work-related accomplishment?

Have you ever had to discipline a problem employee? If so, how did you handle it?

Why do you want this position?

Why are you the best person for this job?

What about Technical writing?

How versatile you are? Can you do other works?

How do you manage time?

How do you handle Conflicts?

What kind of supervisory skills you have?

Any Bad Situation you could not solve?

Anything else you want to say?

About the author:

TOOLS TO PERFORM DIAGNOSTICS AND

REPAIRS OF DESKTOP COMPUTER HARDWARE

I. Memtest: RAM tester: MemTest is a RAM tester that runs under Windows. It verifies that a computer can reliably store and retrieve data from memory.

II. Ribbon Tester: The Ribbon Cable Tester is designed to test the most commonly used flat IDE cables for wiring continuity, opens, shorts and miswiring.

III. PC Cable Tester: It can be used to test BNC; DB15; DB9; DB25; RJ45; USB and IEEE-1394.This cable tester can test the most used data cables, network cables such as printer cable, monitor cable, modem cable, mouse extension cable, game cables, BNC coax cables, RJ45 cables, USB, Firewire etc. for open, shorted, miss-wires, continuity and pin configuration. Auto and manual scans can be selected. Handheld, easy access, simple installation and operation.

IV. Power Supply Tester: tester to perform an automatic PSU test.

V. Multimeter: multimeter can help identify a particular problem quickly and easily by continuity tests on cables and switches and voltage tests.

VI. GFCI Receptacle Tester: to help determine whether electrical RECEPTACLES are providing power and that they are properly wired.

FORM FACTORS OF MOTHERBOARDS

Form factor: Specifies size, shape, and features of a device Determined by motherboard:

I. ATX

II. BTX

III. Micro-ATX (Fits in a set-top or compact/small form factor chassis)

IV. FlexATX

V. NLX

PC POWER SUPPLY COLOR CODES

The color coding is universal amongst all of the power supplies:

    I. Black: Ground

    II. Red: +5V

    III. Yellow: 12V

    IV. Orange: +3.3V

    V. White: -5V (not present on some new supplies)

    VI. Blue: -12V

    VII. Gray: power on indicator

    VIII. Purple: standby power output (not needed for RepRap)

    IX. Green: power on input.

POWER SUPPLY

    I. ATX

ATX has a 20-pin connector for main board power +12, -12, +5, -5, 3.3V output. The on/off switch of ATX units is controlled through the motherboard. ATX is a power supply that has one single plug and socket.

II. AT Power supply

There are 2- 6 pin connectors that supply power to the motherboard.
There are 4 voltages that AT supplies +5, -5 +12, -12.

III. ATX2.0

Instead of 20 pin connectors like the ATX power supply has the ATX 2.0 has a 24 pin connector. In the power supply the computer uses the 3.3 voltages and 5 volt to run the digital circuits. The 12 volt is used to run motors like in the disk drive and the fan to keep the computer from over heating.

IEEE 1394 INTERFACE

I. The IEEE 1394 interface is a serial bus interface standard for high-speed communications and isochronous real-time data transfer

II. It has a data transfer rates of up to 800Mbps, FireWire 800 (IEEE 1394b)

III. IEEE1394b is capable of transfer rates of up to 800Mbps

IV. Maximum data rate of IEEE 1394a is up to 400Mbps

V. The IEEE-1394a interface addresses interconnection of both computer peripherals and consumer electronics

VI. The IEEE-1394a interface provides a throughput ranging from 100 Mbits/sec to 400 Mbits/sec.

VII. IEEE 1394a is a high-speed serial bus standard.

VIII. IEEE 1394, High Performance Serial Bus, is an electronics standard for connecting devices to personal computer.

IX. IEEE 1394 provides a single plug-and-socket connection on which up to 63 devices can be attached with data transfer speeds up to 400 Mbps

X. Maximum data rate of IEEE 1394 200Mbps

RS-232

RS-232 a standard is related to serial data communication. Another name for an RS-232 connection is Serial connection.

It uses these pins:

Pin		Name	Description
I.	1	CD	Carrier Detect
II.	2	RXD	Receive Data
III.	3	TXD	Transmit Data
IV.	4	DTR	Data Terminal Ready
V.	5	GND	System Ground
VI.	6	DSR	Data Set Ready
VII.	7	RTS	Request to Send
VIII.	8	CTS	Clear to Send
IX.	9	RI	Ring Indicator

INTERFACE DONGLES

Dongle is a special cable that provides a connector to a circuit board:

I. PS/2: 6-pin Mini-DIN connector for connecting some keyboards and mice

II. HD15:Video graphics array with three-row 15 pin DE-15 connector

III. 13W3 : 13 total pins, 10 small pins and 3 larger coaxial connectors

IV. USB: This fits into a USB port

V. Serial: RS232 Serial Dongle

UTP

I. Cable type that uses an RJ-45 connector and is most commonly used in an Ethernet network is UTP.

II. Short for unshielded twisted pair, a popular type of cable that consists of two unshielded wires twisted around each other.

III. Due to its low cost, UTP cabling is used extensively for local-area networks (LANs) and telephone connections.

IV. Eight-conductor data cable (CAT 5 UTP) contains 4 pairs of wires in an unshielded plastic sheath.

MONITOR RESOLUTION

Screen resolution signifies the number of dots (pixels) on the entire screen.

Name		x (px)	y (px)
I.	XGA	1024	768
II.	WXGA	1280	720
III.	WXGA	1280	768
IV.	WXGA	1280	800
V.	WXGA	1360	768
VI.	WXGA	1366	768
VII.	XGA+	1152	864
VIII.	WXGA+	1440	900
IX.	SXGA	1280	1024
X.	SXGA+	1400	1050
XI.	WSXGA+	1680	1050
XII.	UXGA	1600	1200
XIII.	WUXGA	1920	1200
XIV.	HDTV	11920	1090

RAID SPECIFICATIONS

RAID levels 3, 4, and 5 use the N+1 formula

Where the capacity of N number of devices will be used for data and the capacity of one of those devices will be dedicated to data protection, or Parity.

Usable + Parity = Raw Capacity

A. Raid 0 (Stripe): Minimum 2 disks, Excellent performance ,No redundancy

B. Raid 1 (Mirror): 2 Drives, High performance, High redundancy, very minimal penalty on write performance.

C. Raid 5 (Drives with Parity): Minimum 3 Drives, Good performance, Good redundancy, Good Price.

D. Raid 6 (Drives with Double Parity): Minimum 4 Drives, Additional fault tolerance.

E. Raid 10 (Mirror+Stripe) or 0+1 (Stripe+Mirror): Minimum 4 Drives, Stripe of mirrors, excellent redundancy, excellent performance. Usable capacity 50% of available disk drives

F. Raid 50 (Parity+Stripe): Minimum 6 Drives. Usable capacity is between 67% - 94%, fast, data redundancy.

G. Raid 60 (Double Parity+Stripe): Minimum 8 Drives, Usable capacity 50% - 88%, fast, extra data redundancy.

SCSI STANDARDS:

SCSI, an acronym for Small Computer System Interface, is a set of protocols and disk I/O signaling specifications

	SCSI Standard	Burst Transfer
I.	SCSI Standard	Burst Transfer
II.	SCSI-15 MB/s	
III.	SCSI-2 (Fast SCSI, Fast Narrow)	10 MB/s
IV.	SCSI-2 Fast Wide (Wide SCSI)	20 MB/s
V.	SCSI-2 Differential Narrow	10 MB/s
VI.	SCSI-2 Differential Wide	20 MB/s
VII.	SCSI-3 Ultra Narrow (Fast-20)	20 MB/s
VIII.	SCSI-3 Ultra Wide	40 MB/s
IX.	SCSI-3 Wide Ultra2	80 MB/s
X.	SCSI-3 Wide Ultra3	320 MB/s

SCSI Parallel Bus Signals

50 Pin Bus (Narrow), 68 Pin Bus (Wide)

Names connector type	Max Speed (MB/s)	Devices	External
I. SCSI-2			
Fast Wide SCSI (Wide SCSI)	20	16	68-pin

II. SCSI-3
Ultra SCSI (SCSI-3, Fast-20, Ultra Narrow)   20   8
    50-pin low density

    50-pin high density

    68-pin

<u>MEMORY MODULES</u>

I. SIMM, SODIMM which of the following are considered RAM types? (Select TWO).

II. DRAM   Dynamic Random Access Memory. This RAM needs constant refreshing or the data stored on it will be lost. Comes in 32 and 64-bit-wide form factors with varying number of chips.

III. SRAM   Static Random Access Memory. Memory that is very fast and very big. Very expensive type of memory. Often seen in CPU caches.

IV. SDRAM   Synchronous Dynamic Random Access Memory. 168 pin for desktops. 68, 144, or 172 pins for Micro DIMM used in laptops

V. RDRAM   RAMBUS Dynamic Random Access Memory. With RAMBUS every slot must be filled either with RIMMs, or with CRIMM (continuity modules). Comes in two sizes: 184-pin for desktops and 160-pin for laptops.

VI. DDR Double Data Rate. For the desktops, this memory had a 184-pin and for laptops had either a 172-pin micro DIMM or 200-pin SO-DIMM.

VII. DDR/2   Double Data Rate. Uses a 240-pin DIMM for desktop and 200-pin for laptops.

VIII. SIMM   Single Inline Memory Module : 30 or 72 pin

DIMM

I. A dual inline memory module (DIMM) consists of a number of memory components that are attached to a printed circuit board.

II. The gold pins on the bottom of the DIMM provide a connection between the module and a socket on a larger printed circuit board.

III. The pins on the front and back of a DIMM are not connected to each other.

IV. SIMMs have a 32-bit data path, while standard DIMMs have a 64-bit data path. DDR Memory modules uses a 168-pin connector.

V. 184-pin DIMMs are used to provide DDR memory for desktop computers.

VI. To use DDR memory, motherboard must have 184-pin DIMM slots and a DDR-enabled chipset.

AGP

I. An AGP (Accelerated Graphics Card) is used to integrate a hardware graphical card to computer's motherboard.

II. The AGP card is a dedicated interface to transfer graphics data. AGP can be classified into different groups based on the speed and signaling voltages

III. Short for Accelerated Graphics Port, an interface specification developed by Intel Corporation. AGP is based on PCI, but is designed especially for the throughput demands of 3-D graphics.

IV. The AGP channel is 32 bits wide and runs at 66 MHz. This translates into a total bandwidth of 266 MBps; as opposed to the PCI bandwidth of 133 MBps. AGP also supports two optional faster modes, with throughputs of 533 MBps and 1.07 GBps. In addition, AGP allows 3-D textures to be stored in main memory rather than video memory.

V. Slot is used for a graphics card   AGP

COMMON TYPES OF NETWORK CABLING

I. CAT3 – 10 Mbit, 16 MHz

II. CAT4 – 16 Mbit, 20 MHz

III. CAT5 – 10/100 Mbit, 100 MHz

IV. CAT5E – 10/100/1000 Mbit, 100 MHz

V. CAT6 – 10/100/1000 Mbit + 10Gbit 55m channel,

    i. (STP), 250 MHz

VI. CAT6A – 10/100/1000 Mbit + 10Gbit UTP and STP, 500 MHz

VII. CAT7 – 10/100/1000 Mbit + 10Gbit, 600 MHz)

VIII. CAT7A – STP, Tera connector, 1 GHz

IX. CAT8 – SOHO, 1200 MHz, 50m channel

X. Twisted-Pair Cable

The pairs are twisted to provide protection against crosstalk, the noise generated by adjacent pairs

XI. Coaxial Cable

Coaxial cable consists of a hollow outer cylindrical conductor that surrounds a single inner wire made of two conducting elements. One of these elements, located in the center of the cable, is a copper conductor. Cable types that use shielding to protect against EMI and RFI   Coaxial.

PROTOCOLS

   I. 10BaseT

  II. 100BaseT (4 pairs CAT4)

 III. 100BaseTX (2 pairs CAT5 – pins 1,2 and 3,6)

 IV. 1000BaseT (4 pairs CAT5E full duplex)

  V. 1000BaseTX (4 pairs CAT6 – 2 pairs Tx

     and 2 pairs Rx)

 VI. 10GBaseT (4 pairs CAT7 full duplex)

DB9

Pin #	DB9 Pin #	Name	Direction	Description
1.	-	-		Protective/Shielded Ground
2.	3	TD	OUT	Transmit Data (Tx, TxD)
3.	2	RD	IN	Receive Data (Rx, RxD)
4.	7	RTS	OUT	Request To Send

5.	8	CTS	IN	Clear To Send
6.	6	DSR	IN	Data Set Ready
7.	5	SGND	-	Signal Ground/Common Return
8.	1	CD	IN	Carrier Detect (DCD)
9.	-	-		Reserved

VGA/SVGA/XGA CONNECTOR PIN-OUT

VGA Connector has 15 pins

VGA/SVGA/XGA Connector Pin-Out

PIN#	SIGNAL DESCRIPTION
1	Red (analog)
2	Green (analog)
3	Blue (analog)
4	Monitor ID Bit2
5	Ground (digital)
6	Ground (red)
7	Ground (green)
8	Ground (blue)
9	not used
10	Ground (sync)
11	Monitor ID Bit0

12	Monitor ID Bit1
13	Horiz Sync
14	Vert Sync
15	not used

CABLE TYPES

I. VGA Cable- a three-row 15-pin connector. VGA connectors and cables carry analog component RGBHV (red, green, blue, horizontal sync, vertical sync) video signals.

II. DVI Cable- (Digital Visual Interface) is a video display interface used to connect a video source to a display device, such as a computer monitor.

III. Ethernet Cable- a thick cable used to connect a computer to a large network.

IV. HDMI Cable- (High-Definition Multimedia Interface) a compact audio/video interface for transferring uncompressed digital audio/video data from an HDMI-compliant device to a compatible digital audio device, computer monitor, video projector, and digital television.

V. XLR Cable- 3-pin. Primarily used to connect microphones to amplifiers for audio.

VI. Coaxial Cable- used as a transmission line for radio frequency signals.

VII. BNC Cable- a miniature quick connect/disconnect RF connector used for coaxial cable.

LATENCY AND RPM

Latency time = (1/ ((Rotational Speed in RPM)/60)) * 0.5 * 1000 mili seconds

HDD Spindle RPM	Average rotational latency [ms]
I. 7,200	4.17
II. 10,000	3.00
III. 15,000	2.00

SAS

Serial Attached SCSI (SAS) is a point-to-point serial protocol that moves data to and from computer storage devices such as hard drives and tape drives.
6 GB/s SAS, Double transfer rate to 6 GB/s, Up to 10m cable lengths

ECC

I. Error Checking and Correction suggests, ECC is technology that allows computers to correct memory errors.

II. The most popular type of ECC used in memory modules is single bit error correction. This enables the detection and correction of single-bit errors (within a byte, or 8bits of data).

III. It will also detect two-bit and some multiple bit errors, but is unable to correct them.

IV. RAM type used to resolve certain memory errors : ECC

BNC

The BNC connector (Bayonet Neill–Concelman) is miniatures quick connect/disconnect RF connector used for coaxial cable.

Cable type required for a BNC connector   Coaxial

PERFORMANCE OF MEMORY

Speed = Width * Frequency

Speed   = Memory Performance (Mb/S)

Width   = Memory Bus (Bits)

Frequency   = Frequency of Data (MHz)

DDR2-SDRAM

I. DDR2-SDRAM is high-performance main memory. Over its predecessor, DDR-SDRAM, DDR2-SDRAM offers greater bandwidth and density in a smaller package along with a reduction in power consumption.

II. In addition DDR2-SDRAM offers new features and functions that enable higher a clock rate and data rate operations of 400 MHz, 533 MHz, 667 MHz, and above. DDR2 transfers 64 bits of data twice every clock cycle. DDR2-SDRAM memory is not compatible with current DDR-SDRAM memory slots.

III. Memory modules that uses a 240-pin connector DDR2.

NORTHBRIDGE/SOUTHBRIDGE CHIPSET ARCHITECTURE

I. Northbridge is the chip or chips that connect a CPU to memory, the PCI bus, Level 2 cache and AGP activities.

II. The Northbridge chips communicate with the CPU through the FSB.

III. The Northbridge chip is one of two chips that control the functions of the chipset.

IV. The Northbridge can consist of more than one discrete chip while the Southbridge is typically only one discrete chip.

V. Chipsets responsible for controlling the data flow between the RAM and the processor

VI. Northbridge: Chipset used by the CPU to communicate with the system memory

VII. A Southbridge chipset handles all of a computer's I/O functions, such as USB, audio, serial, the system BIOS, the ISA bus, the interrupt controller and the IDE channels.

World Wide Name (WWN)

A World Wide Name, or WWN, is a 64-bit address used in fibre channel networks to uniquely identify each element in a Fibre Channel network. Soft Zoning utilizes World Wide Names to assign security permissions.

The use of World Wide Names for security purposes is inherently insecure, because the World Wide Name of a device is a user-configurable parameter.

For example, to change the World Wide Name (WWN) of an Emulex HBA, the users simply need to run the `elxcfg` command.

WWN = World Wide Name

WWPN = World Wide Port Name

WWNN = World Wide Node Name.

WWPN is the number reference the traffic to a particular

port of the HBA.

WWNN is for whole HBA. If it's a dual port HBA

connecting to the SAN, WWPN must be used.

PORTS

FTP 21, TELNET 23, SMTP 25, TFTP 69, HTTPS 443

REMOTE DESKTOP 3389

IPCONFIG

I. Displays all current TCP/IP network configuration values and refreshes Dynamic Host Configuration Protocol (DHCP) and Domain Name System (DNS) settings.

II. Used without parameters, ipconfig displays the IP address, subnet mask, and default gateway for all adapters.

III. Command used to obtain an IP address from the DHCP server   ipconfig/renew

SATA

I. Serial ATA (Advance Technology Attachment)(SATA) is a computer bus interface that connects host bus adapters to mass storage devices such as hard disk drives and optical drives.

II. SATA connections use a 7-pin data cable and 15-pin power cable. SATA and SAS devices use a similar connector

III. Data connector that SATA uses   7-pin

HDMI

I. HDMI (High-Definition Multimedia Interface) is a compact audio/video interface for transferring uncompressed video data and compressed/uncompressed digital audio data from a HDMI-compliant device to a compatible computer monitor, video projector, digital television, or digital audio device.

II. HDMI can provide the highest quality video and audio signal.

III. Higher resolutions, like 1440p and 4K

IV. Faster refresh rates, like 120Hz.

EMI

I. Short for Electromagnetic Interference, EMI is an interference that occurs from invisible magnetic fields. These fields can cause interference in any electric device

II. Common examples of EMI include disturbances in television reception, mobile communication; an electric fan makes the monitor flicker.

III. Example of EMI:Degraded LAN performance due to CAT5 and AC power cables in close proximity

802.11g

802.11g is the third modulation standard for wireless LANs. It works in the 2.4 GHz band (like 802.11b) but operates at a maximum raw data rate of 54 Mbit/s

802.11g has a MAXIMUM speed of up to: 54Mbps

WPA2

Wi-Fi Protected Access II (WPA2 i.e. IEEE 802.11i) is security protocols for wireless communication. It introduces CCMP, a new AES-based encryption mode with strong security.

SMTP

I. Common protocol used to send email

II. Simple Mail Transfer Protocol, a protocol for sending e-mail messages between servers. Most e-mail systems that send mail over the Internet use SMTP to send messages from one server to another

III. The messages can then be retrieved with an e-mail client using either POP or IMAP

IV. SMTP is a core Internet protocol used to transfer e-mail messages between servers.

V. This contrasts with protocols such as POP3 and IMAP, which are used by messaging clients to retrieve e-mail.

USB

Universal Serial Bus (USB) provides an expandable, hot-pluggable Plug and Play serial interface that ensures a standard, low-cost connection for peripheral devices such as keyboards, mice, joysticks, printers, scanners, storage devices, modems, and video conferencing cameras.

The major USB speed improvements are shown on the below timeline.

I.   2014 - USB 3.0 (10 Gbps) 1,250 MBps (proposed)

II. 2008 - USB 3.0 (Super Speed) 625 MBps (current)

III. 2000 - USB 2.0 (HiSpeed) 60 MBps

    USB 2.0 specifications is 480 Mb/sec, 40 times faster than USB 1.1.

IV. 1996 - USB 1.0 (Full Speed) 1 MBps

V.   1996 - USB 1.0 (Low Speed) 0.1 MBps

HYPER-THREADING

I. Intel's Hyper-Threading Technology allows a single physical processor to execute multiple threads (instruction streams) simultaneously, potentially providing greater throughput and improved performance.

II. It improves on the parallelization of computations performed on PC microprocessors.

RAMBUS

The Rambus ® RIMM™ module is a general purpose high-performance memory module suitable for use in a broad range of applications including computer memory, personal computers, workstations, and other applications where high bandwidth and low latency are required.

Maximum speed limit on RAMBUS 800MHz.

MOTHERBOARD FORM FACTORS

Size, Layout, Power, Airflow

BNC

A type of coaxial connector often found on video and digital audio equipment. BNC connectors are normally used to carry synchronizing clock signals between devices. BNCs are bayonet-type connectors rather than screw on or straight plugs.

DB25

A type of D-Sub connector. DB25s are commonly found on computing equipment where they are employed to connect peripherals. TASCAM commonly uses the DB25 connector for analog and/or digital I/O on their products as do some other brands.

Local e-mail clients to retrieve e-mail from a remote server over a TCP/IP connection.

BUS POWER

I. USB cables have wires to carry both power and data. Bus-powered or passive devices get their power from the USB cable.

II. Bus-powered devices are classified as low-powered or high-powered devices depending on the amount of power they draw from the USB bus.

III. Low powered devices use 100 mA or less

IV. High-powered devices use between 100 and 500 mA

TROJAN HORSE

I. It's a Malicious software attached to another piece of software

II. A Trojan horse is a malicious program that is disguised as legitimate software.

III. Trojan horse programs cannot replicate themselves, in contrast to some other types of Malware, like viruses or worms.

IV. A Trojan horse can be deliberately attached to otherwise useful software

VPN

A VPN (Virtual Private Network) provides a secure encrypted tunnel from

A user wants to add an additional network connection to their laptop.

PCMCIA

Personal Computer Memory Card International Association, PCMCIA

CPU CACHE

I. The level 1 (L1) cache resides in CPU

II. A CPU cache is a cache used by the central processing unit of a computer to reduce the average time to access memory.

III. The cache is a smaller, faster memory which stores copies of the data from frequently used main memory locations.

IV. Larger caches have better hit rates but longer latency.

V. Multi-level caches generally operate by checking the smallest level 1 (L1) cache first; if it hits, the processor proceeds at high speed.

VI. If the smaller cache misses, the next larger cache (L2) is checked, and so on, before external memory is checked.

RS232 CABLE PINOUTS

I. RS-232 (Recommended Standard 232) is the standard for establishing serial data signals connection between DTE (Data Terminal Equipment) and DCE (Data Circuit-terminating Equipment).

II. The length of the cable should not exceed 25 feet (about 7.5 meters) unless a signal booster is used.

III. Most commonly used types of serial cable connectors are 9-pin connector DB9 and 25-pin connector DB25.

ZIF SOCKET

I.   The motherboard has a 478-pin zero insertion force (ZIF) socket that supports a single Intel® Pentium® 4 processor.

II. 478 are a 478-contact CPU socket used by some Intel Celeron, Pentium 4, and Pentium 4 Extreme Edition CPU's.

III. Socket-478 supports a 100 MHz, 133 MHz, or 200 MHz Front Side Bus.

IV. The Socket-478 is a Pin Grid Array (PGA) Zero Insertion Force (ZIF) socket.

V.   A ZIF socket features a lever on one side of the socket. When this lever is pulled up, the spring contacts inside the socket are opened.

VI. This allows the CPU to be inserted easily into the socket.

VII. The lever is then pushed down, closing the spring contacts and clamping the CPU into place.

VIII. Short for Zero Insertion Force socket, the ZIF socket was designed by Intel and includes a small lever to insert and remove the computer processor.

IX. Using the lever allows a user to add and remove a computer processor without any tools.

X. All processor sockets from the Socket 2 and higher have been a ZIF socket design.

BOTNET

I. Botnet is a computer infection that allows several computers to launch attacks against a network.

II. It's a Network of autonomous programs capable of acting on instructions.

III. An IRC based, command and control network of compromised hosts (bots)

IV. A bot is a client program that runs in the background of a compromised host

V. It watches for certain strings on an IRC channel

VI. These are encoded commands for the bot

VII. It's used by hackers for DoS, ID Theft, Phishing, key logging, spam

MALWARE

I. Viruses: require the spreading of an infected host file
II. Worms: standalone software, file-transport, a worm self-replicates but a virus can not.
III. Trojans: tricked into loading and executing on systems
IV. Bots: automate tasks and provide services
V. Spyware: is a malware that captures personal information
VI. Adware, any software that covertly gathers user information

IP ADDRESS CLASSES

I. Class A: 0-127
II. Class B: 128 - 191
III. Class C: 192-223
IV. Class D: 224-238

V.   Class E: 239-255

Class A   A Class A address uses only the first octet to represent the network portion

1 to 126
126 Networks
16,777,214 hosts

Class B   A Class B address uses two octets to represent the network portion

128 to 191

Networks 16,384

65,534 hosts per network

Class C   A Class C address uses three octets to represent the network portion

192 to 223.255.255.255

Networks 2,097,152

Class D   Class D is reserved for multicast addressing

224 to 239.x.x.x

Class E   Class E is reserved for future development

240 to 255.x.x.x

MAC ADDRESS FORMAT

I. A MAC address is also called a physical address because it is physically embedded in the interface.

II. A MAC address is a 6-byte (48-bit) hexadecimal address that enables a NIC to be uniquely identified on the network.

III. The MAC address forms the basis of network communication, regardless of the protocol used to achieve network connection.

IV. MAC addresses are expressed in hexadecimal, only the numbers 0 through 9 and the letters A through F can be used in them.

MULTICAST

I. Multicasting is a mechanism by which groups of network devices can send and receive data between the members of the group at one time, instead of separately sending messages to each device in the group.

II. The multicast grouping is established by configuring each device with the same multicast IP address.

UNICAST

   I. With a unicast address, a single address is specified.
  II. Data sent with unicast addressing is delivered to a specific node identified by the address.
 III. It is a point-to-point address link.

BROADCAST

A broadcast address is at the opposite end of the spectrum from a unicast address.

A broadcast address is an IP address that you can use to target all systems on a subnet or network instead of single hosts. In other words, a broadcast message goes to everyone on the network.

IPV6

   I. IPv6 uses a 128-bit addressing scheme.

  II. An IPv6 address is divided along 16-bit boundaries, and each
16-bit block is converted into a four-digit hexadecimal number and separated by colons.

III. IPv6 address has eight fields and each field contains four hexadecimal digits.

IV. IPv6 address is a 128-bit address: 4 bits per digit * 4 digits per field * 8 fields = 128 bits in an IPv6 address

LOOP BACK ADDRESS

IPv4 reserves 127.0.0.1 as the loopback address. IPv6 has the same reservation.

THE STANDARD PORTS

#	PORT	SERVICES
1	25	SMTP
2	22	SSH
3	110	POP3
4	80	HTTP
5	123	NTP
6	220	IMAP3

7	119	NNTP
8	115	SFTP
9	3389	REMOTE DESKTOP
10	443	SSL
11	23	TELNET
12	69	TFTP
13	143	IMAP
14	443	HTTPS
15	20/21	FTP
16	53	DNS
17	161	SNMP
18	546	DHCP CLIENT
19	389	LDAP
20	137	NETBIOS

TRACERT

I. The TRACERT (Trace Route) command is a route-tracing utility used to determine the path that an IP packet has taken to reach a destination.

II. The TRACERT diagnostic utility determines the route taken to a destination by sending Internet Control Message Protocol (ICMP) echo packets with varying IP Time-To-Live (TTL) values to the destination.

III. Note you can run this utility by typing tracert IPAddress or tracert HostName at the command prompt.

IV. Tracert is used to list all of the hops from a starting point

DSL

I. Digital subscriber line (DSL, originally digital subscriber loop) is a family of technologies that provide Internet access by transmitting digital data over the wires of a local telephone network.

II. The bit rate of consumer DSL services typically ranges from 256 kbit/s to 40 Mbit/s in the direction to the customer (downstream), depending on DSL technology, line conditions, and service-level implementation

QUAD-CORE PROCESSOR

    I. A quad-core processor is a chip with four independent units called cores that read and execute central processing unit (CPU) instructions.

    II. It has four CPU cores operating off one CPU package.

BLUE SCREEN OF DEATH

    I. Blue screen of death (BSoD) is a Microsoft Windows operating system error screen that is displayed to indicate system conflicts and the potential for a crash.

    II. This term gets its name because these critical messages were displayed on a blue screen.

    III. BSoD errors relate to system hardware, temperature, timing, resources, corrupt registries or viruses.

    IV. The BSoD error screen serves as an alert to avert further computer and system damage.

    V. The blue screen of death is also known as a stop error.

    VI. The four primary BSoD components are as follows:

        a) Actual error message

b) Loaded memory modules
c) Unloaded modules with no errors
d) Current kernel debug status

LGA 775

LGA 775, also known as Socket, was an Intel desktop CPU socket.

LGA stands for land grid array. Unlike earlier common CPU sockets, such as its predecessor Socket 478, the LGA 775 has no socket holes; instead, it has 775 protruding pins which touch contact points on the underside of the processor (CPU).

Intel Core 2 Duo uses a LGA775 socket.

LGA 1155

LGA 1155, also called Socket H2, is an Intel microprocessor compatible socket which supports Intel Sandy Bridge and Ivy Bridge microprocessors.

RJ-11

It's important to remember that RJ11 has 6 pins, and you are using the middle four-
Black, Red, Green, Yellow.

RJ-11 is short for Registered Jack-11 and is a four or six wire connection primarily used for telephones and computer modem connectors in the United States.

RJ-45

RJ-45 connector Short for Registered Jack-45, a RJ-45 is an 8-pinconnection used for Ethernet network adapters.

TRANSMISSION CIRCUITS

3 main types of transmission circuits (channels), simplex, half duplex and full duplex.

I. Simplex

Data in a simplex channel is always one way, it is not possible to send back error or control signals to the transmit end. An example of a simplex channel in a computer system is the interface between the keyboard and the computer.

II. Half Duplex

A half duplex channel can send and receive, but not at the same time.

III. Full Duplex

Data can travel in both directions simultaneously.

PIN COUNTS

Name	Pin count
I. RS-232	2 (or 4 with HW handshake)
II. RS-422	1
III. RS-485	2 RS-485 interface will usually use pins 7 and 8 for the two data lines
IV. I2C	2
V. SPI	3+1(Additional pins needed for every slave)
VI. Microwire	3+1(Additional pins needed for every slave)

FULL-DUPLEX

It's the ability to transmit data in both directions simultaneously.
Full duplex reduces packet losses.

ECC

I. ECC memory technology will check for and correct single bit errors.

II. Error-correcting code memory (ECC memory) is a type of computer data storage that can detect and correct the most common kinds of internal data corruption. ECC memory is used in most computers where data corruption cannot be tolerated under any circumstances, such as for scientific or financial computing.

III. ECC memory maintains a memory system immune to single-bit errors: the data that is read from each word is always the same as the data that had been written to it, even if a single bit actually stored, or more in some cases, has been flipped to the wrong state.

PXE

I. Preboot Execution Environment (PXE) is used by computers to boot over network.

II. PXE is an open industry standard supported by a number of hardware and software vendors. PXE works with Network Interface Card (NIC) of the system by making it function like a boot device.

III. The PXE-enabled NIC of the client sends out a broadcast request to DHCP server, which returns with the IP address of the client along with the address of the TFTP server, and the location of boot files on the TFTP server.

LPR PORT

I. LPR: Line Printer Remote. Refers to the process that sends jobs to the printer or print queue.

II. The Line Printer Daemon protocol/Line Printer Remote protocol (or LPD, LPR) is a network protocol for submitting print jobs to a remote printer.

SERIAL/PARALLEL COMMUNICATIONS

I. Parallel communication is a method of conveying multiple binary digits (bits) simultaneously; an 8-bit parallel channel will convey eight bits (or a byte) simultaneously.

II. Serial communication is the process of sending data one bit at a time, sequentially, over a communication channel or computer bus.

DEFRAGMENTATION

I. When we create and delete files and applications on computer the hard drive will become fragmented. Data is split into chunks and stored in different areas of the hard disk. Defrag frees up disk space and speeds up computer.

II. In the maintenance of file systems, defragmentation is a process that reduces the amount of fragmentation. It does this by physically organizing the contents of the mass storage device used to store files into the smallest number of contiguous regions.

III. Defrag is the best option to optimize a computer that is heavily used.

PCI EXPRESS

I. PCIe has a switch that controls several point-to-point serial connections

II. PCI Express maintains software compatibility with PCI but offers 250 MB/s bandwidth per direction per lane.

III. Express x16 allows up to 4 GB/s of peak bandwidth per direction, and up to 8 GB/s concurrent bandwidth. PCI-Express x16

RAM TYPES

I. SRAM: Static random access memory used primarily for cache.

II. DRAM: Dynamic random access memory has memory cells with a paired transistor and capacitor requiring constant refreshing.

III. FPM DRAM: Fast page mode dynamic random access memory.

Maximum transfer rate to L2 cache is approximately 176 MBps.

IV. EDO DRAM: Extended data-out dynamic random access memory. Maximum transfer rate to L2 cache is approximately 264 MBps.

V. SDRAM: Synchronous dynamic random access memory takes advantage of the burst mode concept to greatly improve performance. Maximum transfer rate to L2 cache is approximately 528 MBps.

VI. DDR SDRAM: Double data rate synchronous dynamic RAM Maximum transfer rate to L2 cache is approximately 1,064 MBps

VII. RDRAM: Rambus dynamic random access memory RDRAM memory chips work in parallel to achieve a data rate of 800 MHz, or 1,600 MBps.

VIII. Credit Card Memory: Credit card memory is a proprietary self-contained DRAM memory module that plugs into a special slot for use in notebook computers.

IX. PCMCIA Memory Card: another self-contained DRAM module for notebooks, cards of this type are not proprietary and should work with any notebook computer whose system bus matches the memory card's configuration.

X. CMOS RAM: CMOS RAM is a term for the small amount of memory used by computer and some other devices to remember things like hard disk settings;

this memory uses a small battery to provide it with the power it needs to maintain the memory contents.

XI. VRAM: Video RAM, also known as multiport dynamic random access memory (MPDRAM), is a type of RAM used specifically for video adapters or 3-D accelerators.

RDRAM

I. 800MHz   Which of the following is the MAXIMUM speed of RDRAM?

II. RDRAM---Rambus RAM

III. It is a very fast different type of DRAM.

IV. Rambus is the company's name. Intel has adopted this RAM for a while.

V. The special RDRAM bus delivers address and control information using an asynchronous block-oriented protocol.

VI. The bus can address up to 320 RDRAM chips and it rated at 1.6 GBps

GRAPHICS

I. Monochrome- two color video- text only with a resolution of 720 x 350

II. Color Graphics Adapter- CGA- four colors- 320 x 200 resolution for graphics, 640 x 200 for two color

III. Enhanced Graphics Adapter- EGA- 16 colors- 320 x 200 graphics, 640 x 350 text

IV. Video Graphics Array- VGA- introduced with the IBM AT form factor motherboards- used an analog signal- 256KB of video memory on board- 16 colors at 640 x 480 or 256 colors at 320 x 200

V. Super Video Graphics Array- introduced by the Video Electronics Standards Association- 65, 536 colors at 640 x 480, 256 colors at 800 x 600 or 16 colors at 1,024 x 768

VI. Extended Graphics Array- IBM's answer to the SVGA, XGA could only use the MCA expansion bus- it also used interlacing, or scanning every other line on each pass- offered the same resolution options as the SVGA

VIDEO MEMORY

I. VRAM (video RAM)

II. MDRAM (multibank DRAM)

III. SGRAM (synchronous graphics RAM)

IV. WRAM (Window RAM)

V. 3D RAM

GRAPHICS

I. AGP

It is an official extension for cards that required more electrical power. It is a longer slot with additional pins for that purpose.

II. 64-bit AGP

A 64-bit channel was once proposed as an optional standard for AGP 3.0

III. Ultra-AGP, Ultra-AGPII

It is an internal AGP interface standard used by SiS for the north bridge controllers with integrated graphics. The original version supports same bandwidth as AGP 8×, while Ultra-AGPII has maximum 3.2GB/s bandwidth.

IV. PCI-based AGP ports

AGP Express

Not a true AGP interface, but allows an AGP card to be connected over the legacy PCI bus on a PCI Express motherboard.

V. AGI

The ASRock Graphics Interface (AGI) is a proprietary variant of the Accelerated Graphics Port (AGP) standard.

VI. AGX

The EpoX Advanced Graphics eXtended (AGX) is another proprietary AGP variant.

VII. XGP

The Biostar Xtreme Graphics Port is another AGP variant, also with the same advantages and disadvantages as AGI and AGX. PCIe based AGP ports

VIII. AGR

The Advanced Graphics Riser is a variation of the AGP port used in some PCIe motherboards made by MSI to offer limited backwards compatibility with AGP.

WI-FI SECURITY

WPA2 encryption

WPA2-PSK (Preshared Key) is the strongest and most practical form of WPA for most home users. WPA2 is more secure than WPA because it uses the much stronger AES (Advanced Encryption Standard) protocol for encrypting packets

I. WPA2

Wi-Fi Protected Access 2
Introduced September 2004
Two Versions
Enterprise – Server Authentication 802.1x
Personal – AES Pre-Shared Key
Full implementation of 802.11i

II. WPA2-PSK

Pre-Shared Key Mode
Network traffic encrypted using a 256 bit PMK
User enters key (Pairwise Master Key)
64 hex digits
8-63 Printable ASCII characters
Takes the passphrase, SSID of AP, 4096 iterations of
HMAC-SHA-1

LASER PRINTING PROCESS

   I. Raster Image Processing

  II. Charging

 III. Exposing

 IV. Developing

  V. Transferring

 VI. Fusing

VII. Cleaning

FIBER OPTIC

I. Fiber-optic cable types is not affected by electromagnetic interference.

II. Fiber-optic lines are strands of optically pure glass as thin as a human hair that carries digital information over long distances.

III. They are also used in medical imaging and mechanical engineering inspection.

IV. Fiber optics are long, thin strands of very pure glass about the diameter of a human hair.

V. They are arranged in bundles called optical cables and used to transmit light signals over long distances.

It has following parts:

Core - Thin glass center of the fiber where the light travels

Cladding - Outer optical material surrounding the core that reflects the light back into the core

Buffer coating - Plastic coating that protects the fiber from damage and moisture

VI. Single-mode fibers have small cores (about 3.5 x 10-4 inches or 9 microns in diameter) and transmit infrared laser light (wavelength = 1,300 to 1,550 nanometers).

VII. Multi-mode fibers have larger cores (about 2.5 x 10-3 inches or 62.5 microns in diameter) and transmit infrared light (wavelength = 850 to 1,300 nm) from light-emitting diodes (LEDs).

VIII. Some optical fibers can be made from plastic. These fibers have a large core (0.04 inches or 1 mm diameter) and transmit visible red light (wavelength = 650 nm) from LEDs.

FUNCTION KEYS

I. Keys that act as shortcuts for performing certain functions such as saving files or printing data.

II. Function keys usually are lined along the top of the keyboard labeled F1 through F12. These give you quick access to some useful functions. To activate them, just press the FN button on the keyboard together with the function key to activate the commands.

III. Fn+F7 keys can be used to switch displays

IV. Special function key, the Fn key is used in combination with other keys like a Shift key, giving those keys multiple purposes

BLUETOOTH

I. Bluetooth network is used to connect two devices

with each other by the use of pairing. One can pair

phone with Bluetooth accessories, such as headsets, car kits, or speakers.

II. One of the most common types is a Bluetooth headset for making hands-free calls.

III. Bluetooth Wireless technology for short-range voice and data communication

IV. Host controller resides on Bluetooth hardware accepting communications over the physical bus :radio and air

V. HCI Driver resides on the host accepting communications from higher layer protocols

VI. Uses 2.4 GHz ISM band spread spectrum radio

VII. The low power limits the range of a Bluetooth device to about 10 meters (32 feet)

AUTHENTICATION PROTOCOLS

NT Domain, LDAP, SLDAP and RADIUS

DISK DRIVE POWER CONNECTOR

I. Molex   power connectors provide 5 VDC and 12 VDC to parallel ATA (PATA) drives. Molex offers the 8981 in varying wall thickness, profile heights and slot orientations.

II. The pins come in either the standard (2.13mm) .084" or (2.096mm) .0825" diameter.

III. The surface mounted connectors offer low profiles and space saving features. The housing is made from high temperature material which can withstand vapor phase and IR soldering process.

KVM SWITCH

I. A KVM switch (keyboard, video and mouse) is a hardware device that allows a user to control multiple computers from one or more keyboard, video monitor and mouse.

II. KVM switch emulates a monitor and a PS2 and/or USB keyboard and mouse set. On selection it's replicated on the local console ports allowing us to operate the computer normally.

SERVICE DESK ROLES

   I. Single point of contact for users

  II. Communication to users

 III. Coordination for several IT groups and processes

WINDOWS COMMANDS FOR PC
TROUBLESHOOTING

I. CMD   Command Prompt
II. DEVMGMT.MSC   Device Manager
III. DISKMGMT.MSC   Disk Management Tool
IV. EVENTVWR.MSC   Event Viewer
V. GPEDIT.MSC   Group Policy Editor
VI. IPCONFIG view or modify a computer's IP addresses
VII. SECPOL.MSC   Local Security Policy
VIII. MSCONFIG   Microsoft System Configuration Utility
IX. MSINFO32 Microsoft System Information Tool
X. NSLOOKUP verify that DNS name resolution is working
XI. PING verify basic TCP/IP connectivity to a network host
XII. PERFMON Performance Monitor
XIII. REGEDIT Registry Editor
XIV. SERVICES.MSC Services Snap-In
XV. RSTRUI   System Restore
XVI. TASKMGR   Task Manager

TROUBLESHOOTING AND MAINTENANCE OF DESKTOP HARDWARE

I. Problem identification

II. Gathering Information

III. Developing a Solution(logic, reasoning, elimination and common sense, the purpose is to narrow the possible causes of a concern until the root cause is determined and corrected)

IV. Implementing the Solution

PRINTER TYPES

     I. Impact Printer

    II. Non-Impact Printer

  III. Letter Quality Printer

  IV. Inkjet Printer

    V. Laser Printer

  VI. Dot-Matrix Printer

 VII. Thermal Printer

VIII. Photo Printer

  IX. Portable Printer

    X. All-In-One Printer

  XI. Mirror Printing

SAFE MODE

    I. Safe mode starts Windows with a limited set of files and drivers.

   II. This option uses a minimal set of device drivers and services to start Windows.

  III. Safe Mode with Networking   uses a minimal set of device drivers and services to start Windows together with the drivers that you must have to load networking.

IV. Safe Mode with Command Prompt   is the same as Safe mode, except that Cmd.exe starts instead of Windows Explorer.

RECOVERY CONSOLE

It's a command-line interface that provides administrative tools useful for recovering a system that is not booting correctly.

Commands:

I. BOOTCFG   to modify the contents of the "Boot.ini" file

II. BOOTREC   to initiate boot repair

III. DISABLE   to disables a service or driver

IV. ENABLE   to enables a service or driver

V. **FIXBOOT** utility to rewrite the boot sector code of a disk

VI. **FIXMBR** utility to rewrite the master boot record of a disk

VII. **LISTSVC** to lists all available services and drivers

VIII. **LOGON** to logon to a Windows installation

IX. **MAP** to display all drives, file systems & volumes

BIOS

I. The Basic Input/Output System (BIOS), also known as System BIOS, ROM BIOS or PC BIOS

II. This is the software stored on a chip that is a set of instructions for necessary functions in a computer.

CMOS

I. CMOS is short for Complementary Metal-Oxide Semiconductor. CMOS is an on-board semiconductor chip powered by a CMOS battery inside computers that stores information such as the system time and date and the system hardware settings for your computer.

II. CMOS is the area of memory that stores the BIOS.

III. It has a battery that keeps it powered so that modifications to the BIOS are not lost.

POST

Power-on self-test (POST) is a process performed by firmware or software routines immediately after many digital electronic devices are powered on.

POST a series of basic checks that are performed when your computer turns on to make sure your computer works properly.

POST Phases:

I. Test of core hardware: CPU,CMOS, BIOS etc.

II. Test the video subsystem.

III. Identifies version, manufacturer, and date.

IV. Tests the system memory.

COMPUTER PARTS

I. BIOS Chip   Software used to set up the hardware

II. Case Fan   A fan inside that cool off computer parts.

III. CD-ROM Drive Compact Disc Read-Only Memory

IV. COM Port Windows refer to serial ports as COM ports: COM1, COM2.

V. CPU   Central Processing Unit

VI. Hard Disk   Digital data storage device. Holds all the information.

VII. Hardware   Component devices

VIII. Heat Sink   Transfers generated heat

IX. Memory RAM   Form of computer data storage.

X. Motherboard   is the "mother" of all components attached to it.

XI. Operating System An operating system (OS) is a collection of software that manages computer hardware resources and provides common services for computer programs.

XII. Parallel Port for connecting various peripherals.

XIII. PCI slot   Holds PCI Card

XIV. Peripheral   Device attached to a host computer.

XV. Power Supply   Supplies direct current power to all other parts of a computer.

XVI. Serial Port   Serial communication interference

XVII. Software   The programs

XVIII. USB Port   Universal Serial Bus (USB) connects computers & peripherals

OSI

Open System Interconnection

I. Layer 1-Physical   Access to Media, Bit Stream

II. Layer 2-Data Link   Local Network Host Delivery, Error Control

III. Layer 3-Network   Routing to Destination, Switching

IV. Layer 4-Transport   Delivery and Sequencing

V. Layer 5-Session   Establishing Connection, Authentication

VI. Layer 6-Presentation   Encryption and Formatting, Compression

VII. Layer 7-Application   Data Generation, Message Format

DEVICE MANAGER ERROR CODES

The Device Manager is a Control Panel applet in Microsoft Windows operating systems. It allows users to view and control the hardware attached to the computer.

I.	Code 1	the device is not configured correctly
II.	Code 3	the driver for this device might be corrupted
III.	Code 10	this device cannot start.
IV.	Code 12	this device cannot find enough free resources
V.	Code 14	this device cannot work properly until you restart
VI.	Code 16	Windows cannot identify all the resources this device uses.
VII.	Code 18	Reinstall the drivers for this device.
VIII.	Code 19	Windows cannot start this hardware device
IX.	Code 21	Windows is removing this device.
X.	Code 22	this device is disabled.
XI.	Code 24	this device is not present, is not working properly

XII. Code 28   the drivers for this device are not installed.

XIII. Code 29   this device is disabled

XIV. Code 31   this device is not working properly

XV. Code 32   a drivers for this device has been disabled.

XVI. Code 33   Windows cannot determine which resources are required

XVII. Code 34   Windows cannot determine the settings for this device.

XVIII. Code 35   firmware does not include enough information

XIX. Code 36   this device is requesting a PCI interrupt

XX. Code 37   Windows cannot initialize the device driver for this hardware.

XXI. Code 38   Windows cannot load the device driver for this hardware

XXII. Code 39   Windows cannot load the device driver for this hardware.

XXIII. Code 40   Windows cannot access this hardware

XXIV. Code 41   Windows successfully loaded the device driver for HW

XXV. Code 42   Windows cannot load the device driver for this hardware

XXVI. Code 43   Windows has stopped this device

XXVII. Code 44   an application or service has shut down this hardware device.

XXVIII. Code 45   hardware device is not connected to the computer.

XXIX. Code 46   Windows cannot gain access to this hardware

XXX. Code 47   Windows cannot use this hardware

XXXI. Code 48   the software for this device has been blocked

XXXII. Code 49   Windows cannot start new hardware devices

IRQ

Interrupt request (or IRQ) is a hardware signal sent to the processor that temporarily stops a running program and allows a special program, an interrupt handler, to run instead. Interrupts are used to handle such events as data receipt from a modem or network, or a key press or mouse movement. Every PC has maximum of 16 IRQs and is prioritized according to the importance of the device as:

I. IRQ 0 System Timer - Reserved for internal use
II. IRQ 1 Keyboard - Reserved for keyboard
III. IRQ 2 Cascade - used to imitate IRQ 8 - 15
IV. IRQ 3 Second RS-232 serial port (Windows COM 1)
V. IRQ 4 First RS-232 serial port (Windows COM 2)
VI. IRQ 5 Sound Card or second parallel port (Windows LPT 2)
VII. IRQ 6 Floppy Disk Controller
VIII. IRQ 7 First Parallel port (Windows LPT 1)
IX. IRQ 8 Real-time clock
X. IRQ 9 Open Interrupt
XI. IRQ 10 Open Interrupt
XII. IRQ 11 Open Interrupt
XIII. IRQ 12 PS/2 Mouse
XIV. IRQ 13 Math coprocessor
XV. IRQ 14 Primary ATA controller
XVI. IRQ 15 Secondary ATA controller

Non Technical/ Personal/ HR interview

Bottom Line Job interview?

Bottom-line: You will learn to answer any questions in such a way that you match your qualifications to the job requirements.

Interview Question?

Example response. Try to customize your answers to fit the requirements of the job you are interviewing for.

What are your greatest strengths?

I. Articulate.
II. Achiever.
III. Organized.
IV. Intelligence.
V. Honesty.
VI. Team Player.
VII. Perfectionist.
VIII. Willingness.
IX. Enthusiasm.
X. Motivation.
XI. Confident.
XII. Healthy.
XIII. Likeability.
XIV. Positive Attitude.
XV. Sense of Humor.
XVI. Good Communication Skills.
XVII. Dedication.
XVIII. Constructive Criticism.
XIX. Honesty.
XX. Very Consistent.
XXI. Determination.
XXII. Ability to Get Things Done.
XXIII. Analytical Abilities.
XXIV. Problem Solving Skills.

XXV. Flexibility.
XXVI. Active in the Professional Societies.
XXVII. Prioritize.
XXVIII. Gain Knowledge by Reading Journals.
XXIX. Attention to details.
XXX. Vendor management skills.
XXXI. Excellent Project Management skills.
XXXII. Self-disciplined.
XXXIII. Self-reliant.
XXXIV. Self-starter.
XXXV. Leadership.
XXXVI. Team-building.
XXXVII. Multitasking.
XXXVIII. Prioritization.
XXXIX. Time management.
XL. Can handle multiple projects and deadlines.
XLI. Thrives under pressure.
XLII. A great motivator.
XLIII. An amazing problem solver.
XLIV. Someone with extraordinary attention to detail.
XLV. Confident.
XLVI. Assertive.
XLVII. Persistent.
XLVIII. Reliable.
XLIX. Understand people.
L. Handle multiple priorities.
LI. Build rapport with strangers.

What are your greatest weaknesses?

I. I am working on My Management skills.
II. I feel I could do things on my own in a faster way without delegating it.
III. Currently I am learning to delegate work to staff members.
IV. I have a sense of urgency and I tend to push people to get work done.
V. I focus on details and think thru the process start to finish and sometimes miss out the overall picture, so I am improving my skills by laying a schedule to monitor overall progress.

Had you failed to do any work and regret?

I. I have No Regrets.
II. I am Moving on.

Where do you see yourself five years from now?

I. I am looking for a long-term commitment.
II. I see a great chance to perform and grow with the company.
III. I will continue to learn and take on additional responsibilities.
IV. If selected I will continue rise to any challenge, pursue all tasks to completion, and accomplish all goals in a timely manner.
V. I am sure if I will continue to do my work and achieve results more and more opportunities will open up for me.
VI. I will try to take the path of progression, and hope to progress upwards.
VII. In the long run I would like to move on from a technical position to a management position where I am able to smoothly manage, delegate and accomplish goals on time.
VIII. I want to Mentor and lead junior-to-mid level reporting analysts.
IX. I want to enhance my management experience in motivating and building strong teams.
X. I want to build and manage relationships at all levels in the organization.
XI. I want to get higher degree, new certification.

How Will You Achieve Your Goals?

Advancing skills by taking related classes, professional associations, participating in conferences, attending seminars, continuing my education.

Why are you leaving Your Current position?

I. More money
II. Opportunity
III. Responsibility
IV. Growth
V. Downsizing and upcoming merger, so I made a good, upward career move before my department came under the axe of the new owners.

Why are you looking for a new job?

I have been promoted as far as I can go with my current employer.
I'm looking for a new challenge that will give me the opportunity to use my skills to help me grow with the company.

Why should I hire you?

I. I know this business from ground up.
II. I have Strong background in this Skill.
III. Proven, solid experience and track record.
IV. Highest level of commitment.
V. Continuous education on current technical issues.
VI. Direct experience in leading.
VII. Hands-on experience.
VIII. Excellent Project Management skills.
IX. Demonstrated achievements.
X. Knowledge base.
XI. Communications skills.
XII. Ability to analyze, diagnoses, suggests, and implements process changes.
XIII. Strong customer service orientation.
XIV. Detail oriented, strong analytical, organizational, and problem solving skill.
XV. Ability to interact with all levels.
XVI. Strong interpersonal, relationship management skills.
XVII. Ability to work effectively with all levels, cultures, functions.
XVIII. I am a good team player.
XIX. Extensive Technical experience.
XX. Understanding of Business.

XXI. Result and customer-oriented.
XXII. Strong communication skills.
XXIII. Good Project and Resource management skills.
XXIV. Exceptional interpersonal and customer service skills.
XXV. Strong analytical, evaluative, problem-solving abilities.
XXVI. Good management and planning skills.
XXVII. Good Time Management skills.
XXVIII. Ability to work independently.
XXIX. I've been very carefully looking for the jobs.
XXX. I can bring XX years of experience.
XXXI. That, along with my flexibility and organizational skills, makes me a perfect match for this position.
XXXII. I see some challenges ahead of me here, and that's what I thrive on.
XXXIII. I have all the qualifications that you need, and you have an opportunity that I want. It's a 100% Fit.

Aren't you overqualified for this position?

I. In My opinion in the current economy and the volatile job market overqualified is a relative term.
II. My experience and qualifications make me do the job right.
III. I am interested in a long term relationship with my employer.
IV. As you can see my skills match perfectly.
V. Please see my longevity with previous employers.
VI. I am the perfect candidate for the position.
VII. What else can I do to convince you that I am the best candidate? There will be positive benefits due to this. Since I have strong experience in this ABC skill I will start to contribute quickly. I have all the training and experience needed to do this job. There's just no substitute for hands on experience.

Describe a Typical Work Week?

I. Meeting every morning to evaluate current issues.
II. Check emails, voice messages.
III. Project team meeting.
IV. Prioritize issues.

V. Design, configure, implement, maintain, and support. Perform architectural design. Review and analysis of business reports.
VI. Conduct weekly staff meetings.
VII. Support of strategic business initiatives.
VIII. Any duties as assigned. Implementation.
IX. Monitor and analyze reports. Routine maintenance and upgrades.
X. Technical support.
XI. Deploy and maintain.
XII. Provide day-to-day support as required. Work with customers and clients.
XIII. Documentation.
XIV. Standard operating procedures.
XV. Tactical planning.
XVI. Determine and recommend.
XVII. Plan and coordinate the evaluation.
XVIII. Effective implementation of technology solutions.
XIX. To meet the business objectives.
XX. Participation in budget matters.
XXI. Readings to Keep Abreast Of Current Trends and Developments in the Field.

Are You Willing to Travel?

I. For the right opportunity I am open to travel.
II. I'm open to opportunities so if it involves relocation I would consider it.

Describe the pace at which you work?

I. I work at a consistent and steady pace.
II. I try to complete work in advance of the deadline.
III. I am able to manage multiple projects simultaneously.
IV. I am flexible with my work speed and try to conclude my projects on time.
V. So far I have achieved all my targets
VI. I meet or exceeded my goals.

How Did You Handle Challenges?

I. Whenever the project got out of track I managed to get the project schedules back on the track.
II. Whenever there was an issue I had researched the issues and found the solutions.
III. We were able to successfully troubleshoot the issues and solve the problems, within a very short period of time.

How do you handle pressure? Stressful situations?

I. In personal life I manage stress by going to a health club.
II. I remain calm in crisis.
III. I can work calmly with many supervisors at the same time.
IV. I use the work stress and pressure in a constructive manner.
V. I use pressure to stay focused, motivated and productive.
VI. I like working in a challenging environment.
VII. By Prioritizing.
VIII. Use time management
IX. Use problem-solving
X. Use decision-making skills to reduce stress.
XI. Making a "to-do" list.
XII. Site stress-reducing techniques such as stretching and taking a break.
XIII. Asked for assistance when overwhelmed.

How Many Hours Do You Work?

I enjoy solving problems and work as much as necessary to get the job done.
The Norm is 40 hour week.

Why are you the best person for the job?

I. It's a perfect fit as you need someone like me who can produce results that you need, and my background and experience are proof.
II. As you can see in My resume I've held a lot of similar positions like this one, and hence I am a perfect fit as all those experiences will help me here.
III. I believe this is a good place to work and it will help me excel.

What are you looking for in a position?

I. I'm looking for an opportunity where I may be able to apply my skills and significantly contribute to the growth of the company while helping create some advancement and more opportunities for myself.
II. It seems this organization will appreciate my contributions and reward my efforts appropriately to keep me motivated.
III. I am looking for job satisfaction and the total compensation package to meet My Worth that will allow me to make enough money to support my lifestyle.

What do you know about our organization?

I. This is an exciting place to work and it fits my career goals.
II. This company has an impressive   growth.
III. I think it would be rewarding to be a part of such a company.

What are your short term goals?

I'd like to find a position that is a good fit and where I can contribute and satisfy my professional desires.

What Salary are you looking for?

I. Please provide me the information about the job and the responsibilities involved before we can begin to discuss salary.
II. Please give me an idea of the range you may have budgeted for this position.
III. It seems my skills meet your highest standards so I would expect a salary at the highest end of your budget.
IV. I believe someone with my experience should get between A and B.
V. Currently I am interested in talking more about what the position can offer my career.
VI. I am flexible but, I'd like to learn more about the position and your staffing needs.
VII. I am very interested in finding the right opportunity and will be open to any fair offer you may have.

Tell me more about yourself.

I. I'm an experienced professional with extensive knowledge.
II. Information tools and techniques.
III. My Education.
IV. A prominent career change.
V. Personal and professional values.
VI. Personal data.
VII. Hobbies.
VIII. Interests.
IX. Describe each position.
X. Overall growth.
XI. Career destination.

Why did you leave your previous job?

I. Relocation.
II. Ambition for growth.
III. This new opportunity is a better fit for my skills and/or career ambitions.
IV. To advance my career and get a position that allows me to grow.
V. I was in an unfortunate situation of having been downsized.

VI.   I'm looking for a change of direction.
VII.   I want to visit different part of the country I'm looking to relocate.
VIII. I am looking to move up with more scope for progression.

What relevant experience do you have?

I have these XYZ related experience.
I have these skills that can apply to internal management positions et al.

If your previous co-workers were here, what would they say about you?

Hard worker, most reliable, creative problem-solver, Flexible, Helping

Where else have you applied?

I am seriously looking and keeping my options open.

What motivates you to do a good job?

Recognition for a job well done.

Are you good at working in a team?

Yes.

Has anything ever irritated you about people you've worked with?

I've always got on just fine with all my co-workers.

Is there anyone you just could not work with?

No.

Tell me about any issues you've had with a previous boss.

I never had any issues with my boss.

Do you have any questions?

Please explain the benefits and bonus.
How soon could I start, if I were offered the job?

Why did you choose this career?

    I.   Life style.
   II.   Passion.
  III.   Desire.
  IV.   Interesting.
   V.   Challenging.
  VI.   Pays Well.
 VII.   Demand.

What did you learn from your last job experience?

I gained experience that's directly related to this job.

Why is there a gap in your resume?

Because of Personal and family reasons I was unable to work for some time.
   I.   Unemployed.
  II.   Job hunt.
 III.   Layoffs.

How do you keep current and informed about your job and the industries that you have worked in?

I.   I pride myself on my ability to stay on top of what is happening in the industry.
II. I do a lot of reading.
III. I belong to a couple of professional organizations.
IV. I have a strong network with colleagues.
V.   I take classes and seminars.
VI. I have started and participated in many technical blogs.

Tell me about a time when you had to plan and coordinate a project from start to finish?

I.   I headed up a project which involved customer service personnel and technicians.
II.   I organized a meeting and got everyone together.
III. I drew up a plan, using all best of the ideas.
IV.   I organized teams.
V.   We had a deadline to meet, so I did periodic checks with various teams involved.
VI.   After four weeks, we were exceeding expectations.
VII. We were able to begin implementation of the plan.
VIII. It was a great team effort, and a big success.
IX.   I was commended by management for my managing capacity.

What kinds of people do you have difficulties working with?

I.   I have worked in very diverse teams.
II. Diversity means differences and similarities with men and women from very diverse backgrounds and culture. It helps us grow as a human being.
III. The only difficulty was related to work related dishonesty by a person.
IV. He was taking credit for all the work our team accomplished.

What do you want to be in 5 years?

I hope to develop my management skills by managing a small staff.

Explain an Ideal career for you?

    I.   I would like to stay in a field of ABC.
    II.   I have been good at ABC.
    III.   I look forward to ABC.

What are your job responsibilities?

I would expect expanded responsibilities that could make use of my other skills.

What is your dream job?

Includes all of the responsibilities and duties you are trying to fill.
I also thrive in the fast changing environment where there is business growth.

What skills you have?

I was very pleased to develop the A, B, C skills that you are seeking.

What sets you apart?

    I.   Once I am committed to a job or project I take it with tremendous intensity.
    II.   I want to learn everything I can.
    III.   I am very competitive and like to excel at everything I do.

If the project not gone as planned what action you will take?

Backup and identify precautions.

What you do if you are unable to meet deadlines?

    I.   Negotiate.
    II. Discussion.
    III. Restructure.
    IV. Redefine Optimum goal.
    V. Show a price structure.

Interpersonal skill?

    I.   I had to learn to say no.
    II. Helpful to other staff.
    III. Help in return.

Improve?

In any job I hold I can usually find inefficiencies in a process, come up with a solution.

What do you feel has been your greatest work-related accomplishment?

    I.   Implemented an idea to reduce expenses, raised revenues.
    II. Solved real problems.
    III. Enhanced department's reputation.

Have you ever had to discipline a problem employee? If so, how did you handle it?

Yes.

I did it using:

    I. **Problem-solving skills**
    II. **Listening skills, and**
    III. **Coaching skills**

Why do you want this position?

    I. **I always wanted the opportunity to work with a company that leads the industry in innovative products.**
    II. **My qualifications and goals complement the company's mission, vision and values.**
    III. **I will be able to apply and expand on the knowledge and experience, and will be able to increase my contributions and value to the company through new responsibilities.**

Why are you the best person for this job?

    I. **I have extensive experience in XYZ (Skill they are looking for)**
    II. **I'm a fast learner.**
    III. **I adapt quickly to change.**
    IV. **I will hit the ground running.**
    V. **I'm dedicated and enthusiastic.**
    VI. **I'm an outstanding performer.**
    VII. **I may be lacking in this specific experience but I'm a fast learner and I'll work harder.**

What about Technical writing?

    I. **I can convert any complex technical information into simple, easy form.**
    II. **I can write reports to achieve maximum results.**

How versatile you are? Can you do other works?

I am flexible and can adapt to any changing situations.

How do you manage time?

   I. I am very process oriented and I use a systematic approach to achieve more in very less time.
   II. I effectively eliminate much paperwork.

How do you handle Conflicts?

   I. I am very tactful;
   II. I avoid arguments and frictions and
   III. I establish trust and mutual understanding.

What kind of supervisory skills you have?

I. I make sure that everyone understands their responsibilities.
II. I try to be realistic in setting the expectations and try to balance the work among all.

Any Bad Situation you could not solve?

I've never yet come across any situation that couldn't be resolved by a determined, constructive effort.

Anything else you want to say?

   I. I am excited and enthusiastic about this opportunity
   II. I am looking forward to working with you.

About the author:

/editor/compiler:
Kumar is an author, educator, and an IT professional and he enjoys sharing his expertise on wide variety of subjects in easy language to help all his readers.